A WILTED FLOWER IN YOUR WATERED GARDEN

DONALD SEARS II

authorHOUSE®

AuthorHouse™
1663 Liberty Drive
Bloomington, IN 47403
www.authorhouse.com
Phone: 1 (800) 839-8640

Published by AuthorHouse 12/13/2016

ISBN: 978-1-5246-5444-3 (sc)
ISBN: 978-1-5246-5443-6 (e)

Print information available on the last page.

CONTENTS

A Feather
September 10, 2016

Gleefully taken apart by the desires of the great mongrecycle is a fishing trip to the zoo.

The last thing it saw was a deep blue sorcery.

But that doesn't exactly score the team playing hopscotch on an angry sea.

Hold up your hand if you feel something akin to an eyelash or a backlash of time.

There's not much to get ready for except a storm blowing in the back of my mind.

Sir Lancelot is in a cheap motel with Queen Guenevere and they are making adult films to hand down to future generations but not yet.

As you will surely see when you have grown in wisdom and in fortune the melting pot is itself a little soupy and has simmered for centuries.

Someday we will be able to travel back in time and learn card tricks from Merlin the Magician.

We all know the hand is quicker than the eye but I learned the hard way a fist in the eye is instantaneous.

When will we take apart a trip to Michigan? That's a good question and there's an even better answer but I don't know what it is. And where is a good glass of sour mash and potatoes when you need them? Making whiskey is an even better trade to sharpen your blade.

True love is beginning to show through the darkness of simplicity and I stopped growing yesterday which is a feather in my nap.

A Penny For My Thoughts
1973

On a walk on a city street
I found a penny at my feet
I tossed it down a wishing well
I wished it well and listened as it fell
I never heard a sound
Then I knew that I had found
You are a part of my soul
And part of me knows
I'll never let you go

On a tree I see cherries
By a stream I pick strawberries
I lie in a field of clover
I watch the clouds pass over

In a forest by my fire
As the moon climbs ever higher
I cast my spirit into the sky
My fire snaps and hot sparks fly
Then a star falls down to me
It wanted to be free
I wish and listen for a sound
Stars seldom touch the ground
That star fell just for you
Did you see that same star too?

When I reminisce of all I've left behind
It may dawn on you like eyesight to the blind
If I made a list of all I have missed
A list of everything we used to do
Do you miss those same things too?

On a tree, I see cherries
By a stream, I pick strawberries
I lie in a field of clover
I watch clouds pass over

A Place In the Woods
December 1, 2012

There was a place in the woods
We kids would congregate there
A place to learn things all kids should
We learned to smoke and drink and swear

Roland was a boy I knew
He'd bring a pint of wine
Pressed from grapes that grew
On his family's vines

We passed the bottle back and forth
We talked the afternoon away
Before we replaced the cork
The sun had set on two boys at play

I never asked if the drink was stolen
Or a gift from his dad
I was afraid if I asked Roland
I would spoil the good times we had

A Song of Youth

November 2, 2016

I reflect on times when I was younger
There was a spell that I went under
I walked around the woods all day
At night I searched a different way

Nature was my friend back then
I could build a fire in the rain and wind
A lean-to was my home a while
When it was cold I learned to smile

I wrote and sang a song of youth
I thought I knew some profound truth
I was in a pretty decent mood
When I grew my own food

I now find myself in elder years
My mortgage payment interferes
I have no hut, a house instead
At night I sleep in a warm bed

Porch sitting after mowing grass
I reminisce my long gone past
No large regrets am I remembering
To my future I am now surrendering

ALARM CLOCK
OCTOBER 1, 2012

I have an alarm clock
In a drawer with my socks
It doesn't wake me in time
I want to go out
I'm not on a bus route
I can't take a cab for a dime

My girlfriend's crazy
Her memory's hazy
She shops for secondhand clothes
She's complicated
Says she's a native
She wears fishnet hose

We went to a party
Wine, cheese and arty
They had me arrested again
Got in a contest
I won all bets
With five flatulent men

I want to be like Granddad
He had a flat head
He was dropped on it at birth
Combed his hair straight up
Wore Grandma's makeup
They joined the Catholic Church

All O' God's Kitties
2013

They may be large or small
They may be calico
Or white as a cotton ball
They may be indigo

But all o' God's kitties got soul

Their breed may be mixed
They may be young or old
They may have been fixed
Or have been bought or sold

But all o' God's kitties got soul

They may have caught rats
They may wear collars of gold
They may be shelter cats
Or survive the rain and snow

But all o' God's kitties got soul

They may have eyes of blue
They may win at cat shows
Or lie around with little to do
They may be meek or bold

But all o' God's kitties got soul

BOURBON & BLUES
1984

A bottle of bourbon
And that old blues guitar
A bottle of bourbon
And that old blues guitar
I'm drinkin' more'n I'm earnin'
In this crosstown bar

Shot glasses ringin'
Out the beat like a chime
Shot glasses ringin'
Out the beat like a chime
I'll keep on singin'
If you toss me a dime

My baby's out runnin'
I'm drinkin' alone
My baby's out runnin'
I'm drinkin' alone
That guitar keeps strummin'
Why don't she come back home

That guitar keeps dronin'
That slow mournful sound
That guitar keeps dronin'
That slow mournful sound
Sings I miss that woman
When she ain't around

Got nuthin' to lose
Got nuthin' to gain
Got nuthin' to lose

Got nuthin' to gain
Cold bourbon & blues
Helps ease the pain

If you're born to win, you never lose
If you're born to win you never lose
Fill my shot glass again
I's born to sing the blues

All Possible Hues
November 17, 2012

The innocence of a rare flower
Blooming in May
The Good Lord looks upon us
In much the same way

The green grass and trees
And all living things
Are all one with God
And other human beings

Our earth radiates with life
And this is a device God may use
To decorate our world
With all possible hues

All beauty begins at heaven's gates
Beyond heaven's shore
There his love waits
Forevermore

Angels Aren't Sent to Paradise
2013

Angels aren't sent to paradise
Or to parties, sugar and spice
They aren't dispatched to joyful lands
They go to fill empty hands

Have you seen one, do you know
To help you through fog and snow?

Angels are sent for their influence
To broken hearts that aren't congruent
Sacred vows may be blown
Angels may lead them home

Have you seen one, do you know
To help you through fog or snow?

Do you remember your worst day?
You wish the world would go away
But next day when things are right
An angel spent the night

Have you seen one, do you know
To help you through fog or snow?

You may say they're hard to find
Or that they are in my mind
But from my point of view
I've seen quite a few

Answerin' Machine

February 20, 2014

In a downtown bar, I was drinkin' alone
In a downtown bar, I was drinkin' alone
I heard my little Bunny luvin'
With another man over the phone

In a downtown bar I was drinkin' alone
In a downtown bar, I was drinkin' alone
I heard my little bunny luvin'
With another man over the phone

When I call my Bunny, I get her answerin' machine
When I leave my number, Bunny don't call me

I come home last Friday night
I say, I come home last Friday night
To a sight that made this cowboy's poor heart break
I seen a city dude eatin' my Bunny's carrot cake

When I call my Bunny I get her answerin' machine
When I leave my number, Bunny don't call me

SWEET MANDY
2013

Sweet Mandy's got holes in her shoes
Sweet Mandy's got holes in her shoes
It makes her Daddy whimper
Her feet get cold in winter

If I was a rich man we would go to Monaco
If I was a rich man we would go to Monaco
In the summer she'd wear stylish shoes
In the winter she'd wear warmer boots

Sweet Mandy dances to my songs
Sweet Mandy dances to my songs
She sings, "Daddy, nuthin's wrong"

I fixed her shoes the best that I could
I fixed her shoes the best that I could
I had no cash for leather
Cardboard in cold weather

Sweet Mandy's got holes in her shoes
Sweet Mandy's got holes in her shoes
It makes her Daddy whimper
Her feet get cold in winter

Sweet Mandy dances to my songs
Sweet Mandy dances to my songs
She sings, "Daddy, nuthin's wrong"
She sings, "Daddy, nuthin's wrong"

At Seven: Forty-Five PM
March 26, 2016

When I reminisce, a song is forming
When you awake in the glow of morning
And when we lie down in the late evening
Always then am I believing
At night our love is our adorning

You're like a gazelle or a doe of the field
With your sweet taste all love is revealed
You're the most lovely of all the world's women
My soul's on a journey to your attention
And when you smile all suffering is healed

You give so much while so little you take
And when we're apart all my bones ache
Your scent lingers like a bush of roses
And I long for you as evening closes
All thoughts are of you at a quarter to eight

BACK SEAT BASS GUITAR BLUES
2013

Woke up this mornin' 'fore the early early light
Woke up this mornin' 'fore the early early light
Can't remember Mama's face I was so damn tight
Got nuthin' I can do but play it in the back
And hope she returns by the dawn's early early crack

Woke up this mornin' back seat of my car
Woke up this mornin' back seat of my car
Realized I'd been huggin' my bass guitar
Got nuthin' I can do, but play it in the back
Hopin' sweet Mama returns by the dawn's early early crack

Woke up this mornin' couldn't find dry land
Woke up this mornin' couldn't find dry land
Here comes sweet Mama with a wine bottle in 'er hand.
All I can do is play it in the back
Sweet Mama returned by the dawn's early early crack

Bottle Of Accidents
January 2, 1977

"How many times must I be?" he asked his sky full of pillow cases. They only stared back and wondered where they were going, although it was plain to see they weren't going anywhere. It was then it returned to this other than looking into it from where it was. So sneaking up from behind him from where I was hiding in his shadow, I told him a story I knew. And so he said, "I see you are wrong, so cross your ear with a bucket of beer."

I exclaimed, "My what, are you God or a priest!"

"It's none of your life, are you spent? He answered.

So I knew He was guessing my game. I handed Him my umbrella due to a cloud in the back of my mind, and returned His watch I'd stolen. I then climbed back into my bottle of accidents that I use to keep myself from knowing too much, and I told Him to try that again. This was so I could catch Him off guard and discover the identity of His watchdog because this all happened long after you were born.

And after all, I didn't really care about His watchdog at all if you sort out all the loose particles and draw a map. Anyway, so partly because all the was giggled at its fictitious parody. And I knew I must escape from my bottle of accidents but I couldn't get out without letting my mistakes go. So do you know what I did? What would you have done? I stayed right there until I realized I was too ho hummed on it. Maybe if I created something far too less apt to be unlikely than its natural resourcefulness, the answer would come to me in some mysterious way. This gave me enough time to forget the question, so I realized I was free from my bottle of mistakes. I had simply stayed there until I had forgotten about it. Do you know why?

Because tomorrow's in the back
Of a long list of jokes,
And it looks like it likes all of its friends,
You should start in before it begins.

That was all wrong because I don't remember what I was doing before I said it, but from my past I knew all of the pieces were missing, but from what? So naturally I knew it was time to forget the entire thing since I already know how it ended. (I do feel very sorry for you since I already know how it ended) because you do too.

BUTTER AND HONEY
APRIL 4, 2012

God brings up waters from the rivers
And his glory overflows the banks
Even one who's a beginner
They're experienced to give him thanks

For milk we give we will eat butter
For butter we will eat honey
Give freely and don't mutter
All we give will feel good in our tummie

His wings span all children, women and man
The Lord touches our deeper emotions
We began from nothing but his hands
He sparked our universal explosion

Jesus Christ is a man to consider
Did he know as he suffered on the cross
That later this scene would get bigger
And he'd die for all souls who are lost?

CABIN FEVER
JANUARY 15, 2014

Below zero six days in a row
Twelfth of December, the thermostat's low
Sugar, share these quilts and make it nice
It's another day in paradise

Cabin fever, cabin fever, my Honey keeps me well
Sweet Baby's my medicine
I want to run and yell!

Furnace is old, no cash to replace it
Honey it's cold so let us face it
We have little heat but the body kind
Tell me a joke, I'm losing my mind

Your eyes sparkle like two sapphires
I may be old but I'm not ready to retire
Get ready to go around twice
It's another day in paradise

Cabin fever, cabin fever, my Honey keeps me well
Sweet Baby's my medicine
I want to run and yell!

CHASING AFTER WIND
1999

I'm vexed by my own wisdom
My knowledge brings me sorrow
All my work is only vanity
Like my vision of tomorrow

I work to earn my money
And with that money buy
More of life's possessions
That I'll leave here when I die

All I do has been done
All I know has been known
But wisdom excels folly
By God's light a tree has grown

I look to wisdom of the past
To see what future it will bring
But what can any mortal do
Who came before the King?

Rich folks gather wealth
It's more than they can spend
This too is only vanity
And they're chasing after wind

For everything there's a season
Every matter has its time
To be born and die under heaven
There is reason and a rhyme

There is a time to be silent

And a time to speak
There's a time to be sought
And there's a time to seek

There is a time to kill
A time for war and peace
A time to laugh and to heal
A time to mourn and weep

There is a time to love and hate
A time to keep and throw away
And every time the sun rises
It's time to greet another day

Then there is toil for envy
To this there is no end
For one's envy of another
Is also chasing after wind

Two are better than the one
If one falls they're lifted by the other
But woe to one that falls alone
Without a sister or a brother

If one lies down alone
One will freeze in winter storms
But if the two lie down together
One will keep the other warm

There's nothing new beneath the sun
All there is has always been
So all but true love is vanity
And chasing after wind

CAFFEINE
AUGUST 22, 2016

I wake up in the morning
Like I awake from a coma
Life seems flat then and boring
Until I smell that aroma

I turn on the pot
I wait for my brew
I always make a lot
It's for me and it's for you

Caffeine harms the kidneys
I have a stone like Gibraltar
It can't be cured with surgeries
Or so says Doctor Walker

I don't smoke a pipe
Or have alcohol in my drink
It is my only vice
And my breath don't stink

CLARISSA
NOVEMBER 2, 2013

The lady's name was Clarissa
She always spoke her mind
Clarissa wanted children
And a husband on the dotted line

It was a charming spot
They picnicked beneath a maple tree
She was with her boyfriend, Scott
And he got down on one knee

"My sweet, let us take this course:
Clarissa, love, I leave it to you
If we never marry, there will be no divorce
No one will ever sue"

"Scott, I'd take a rattlesnake from you
Before an engagement ring
You'll use me 'till you're through
And leave me without a thing"

23

CLEOPATRA
1987

"Where have I been asking?" Joseph the Mule-driver asked.

"Well uh believe me it ain't music!" cried the driver, "Music drives the soul to tears! I hear it crying music!"

Dropping an unusual set of events is ever composing. Driftwood matters here. Be beautiful with me. Be like another dream. When you were young we went on journeys. Magic moments no one knows. We're here in our own mind now...I mean, supposing we're only guessing and we are. "Who says?" I asked.

"The moon knows the truth, shining down on us all; just another ancient mystery. Who all knows you? Dreams are all there is here, just dreams that drift away on moonbeams. Take my hand and take me with you through all your dreams. Be like that again, go with me, let me take you with me to the stars. We're all gone here. It's an ancient secret no one knows and deep down inside we all know it. It's like being young and full of life and music and old and full of wisdom at the same time. You're both so full of magic and moondust, talking to spirits and the moon and all. Open up to me. I want to be your friend. Take me through all your dreams and I'll take you to the outside corners of another universe. Don't be angry and tired of life. Life has its surprises. Your dreams mean more than money.

Now you see it's more than the unlikely truth to be seen. Respectable and sure and new and simple and undreamweavable. Several times tonight I've taken it upon myself, but surely. I'm a misty-eyed fool, Bro. Not nearly as nervous though. Several surely to be angry with me now and never. But exactly not necessarily so. It's so touch and go that materialistically speaking, who knows and who cares? What if we do and whom do we if we do? Not me if it's you and so do you and don't we all sometimes?"

Cleopatra was really there, watching me above all else. Magnificent in her splendor she walked across the Nile to get to some far distant reality of love. We were there like some ancient melodrama holding hands and watching the sunrise. Far above some not-too-distant awakening of some simple truth laid the two of us in the tall grasses.

And we lived happily ever after.

The End

COME TO THE LORD WITH JOY
MARCH 18, 2014

The Holy Spirit is like many waters
Seeing us through our darkest nights
Leading us places where seas are calmer
Like a rainbow disperses a spectrum of light

Come home to Lord Jesus with thanksgiving
Sing songs of praise to salvation
He destroys death and keeps us living
Let's reach with our voices to heaven

Unlike the gods, our God creates plans
The seas have known him since their birth
The hills are his and he formed dry land
Then he gave us gifts like our universe

O Heavenly Father, you bring inspiration
My prayers have brought on a change
You see me through trying situations
I pray to you in Jesus' name

DUST IN THE MIST

JANUARY 26, 2011

Divine blood is turned to wine
The bread is of immaculate birth
Come to Christ's table and dine
Drink from his cup, end your search

There is no need to travel 'round
Just be yourself
He'll visit if we are home bound
And give blessings for our health

Though this occurred in the past
Father God and Son still exist
In their army where first is last
You and I can still enlist

EVERLASTING LIFE
JUNE 1, 2004

Don't be downcast and dejected
When he who speaks the truth
Has appeared unveiled among you
And his every word is his truth

In this day the beginning is the end
And that end is the beginning of this day
Motion has been generated by the Almighty
That sweeps our desires away

Come taste the water of everlasting life
Wash sorrow away from your hearts
That his divine secret may be known to you
Read the message the Good Lord imparts

All possessing all knowing protector
Of the souls of every woman and man
If a trial pursues and overtakes me
Please rest beside me at my right hand

Every Seed that's Forever Sown
2014

O God, I am your poor creature
Please cure my ignorance and be my teacher
Then be the rock on which I stand
To spread your love across this barren land

Please bless my heart with your sweet mercy
From my darkest nights to mornings early
Lord, illuminate my spirit, make it glow
With your beauty that helps the orchids grow

You transformed my poverty to treasure
Like a speck of dust to the universe unmeasured
Each snowflake is individually your own
As is every seed that's forever sown

FATHER'S DAY
JANUARY 7, 2016

All fathers are equal
Although nothing can be said for all
Some are rich and some are poor
And some don't heed the call

He may lead the mealtime prayer
He may have passed away
Grandchildren may come to visit
When he is old and gray

Some children are adopted
They are special girls and boys
Because their fathers have them
Entirely by choice

To some kids it's the simple things
And he's the best on earth
If he brags on them
And shows them off at work

To make all fathers equal
It takes time to reflect
And to give them
Our love and our respect

FEELING YOUR AGE
1988

Old house, you are feeling your age
But you are glad to be alive
You're at peace with your many spirits
And people who find respite within you
From the hypocrisy and sham
Of the daily world

Old house, your plaster is cracking
But I can still rest here for a while
Your walls reflect searching and wisdom
You are old but you still
Can give birth to new spirit

Old house, so many come to you
Who have been rejected before
But you throw open your door
Like the arms of a mother
Who loves all of her children
You are one with the earth
Your energy will live on
Long after your walls are gone

FISHING WHILE IT SNOWS
JANUARY 11, 2015

When I'm feeling down and out
And I have the blues
I might go and fish for trout
That often keeps me amused

While standing in a mountain stream
I'm warm and dry in waders
Like Dad taught when I was thirteen
I'd like some fish to eat with taters

I don't bother tuna while they spawn
At my fishing spot where know one knows
I've practiced casting on my lawn
The fish aren't biting while it snows

Before I go I check my satchel
I make sure there is bait
Hooks and sinkers in my tackle
To land a bass would sure be great!

FLY HOME
APRIL 18, 2016

Open up and reply
And wish you could fly
Without a ticket
Like a quail in a thicket

Would you fly home
And there be alone?
There is so much to say
It can't be said in one day

Make a wish on a page
And don't be afraid
Send a note in a bottle
Like a plane's open throttle

If you could fly—
Birds do not try
They don't argue, they do
It can happen to you

Forever Bright

July 4, 1984

Reflecting on ancient lore
The Gospels were carried to distant shores
And people knocked on those doors
They kept their candle burning bright
In the catacombs at night
And brought more folks into the light
Through storms of opposition in the early days
What kept them on their weary way?

Could only ancient dreams and fear
Fill our hearts after all these years
And overflow our cup with love
Without the light from above?

Reflecting and turning pages
How has it shone down through the ages?

To help lift the low of heart
To inspire great works of art
To touch those deep in despair
To teach us to love and share

It's the poor in spirit and those who mourn
The pure of heart; they are reborn
And those who need a helping hand
In their hearts they understand...

Christ, who taught the virtue of forgiving
And lived the life and kept it living
Those who believed and were convicted
Just as the Good Lord predicted

For those who live beneath the light
And keep it good and keep it right
The candle burns forever bright

FROSTY FLOWERS
2010

O the pangs of loneliness
When my life was untouched
To a time when love is given freely
Based on honesty and trust

From the reaches of creation
To the blood that flows through veins
From the healing power of prayer
Go mysteries unexplained

The faithful of the world
While scripture's being read
Like frosty flowers in autumn
We solemnly bow our heads

The sun that lights the earth
Creates both fire and rain
But the light of our spirit
Is a mystery unexplained

GOD CAME TO THE WORLD
JANUARY 25, 2013

God came to the world to learn of our lives
A little compassion was sure hard to find
He didn't get angry but he paced back and forth
He paced west to east then he paced south to north

When he had the earth entirely surveyed
The Lord reached conclusions of changes to be made
Nothing profound had to be done
He made acts of giving much more fun

Contributions of gold, even second hand shirts
When given to the poor, they gain in worth
The money we've made won't pass heaven's gates
Spread the good word, your reward waits

Let's not be tight with all of our wealth
The people we're saving might be ourselves
Little is certain but the sun, moon and stars
How did they find out where you are?

GOD LOVES HIS CRITTERS
MARCH 4, 2014

God loves all of his critters
So to Noah, he gave a call
He said, "When you build your ark
Be sure and save two of all!

Critters possess no sin
They do what animals do
And they don't know any better
When they take a bite out of you

You may see them as inferior
Like folks who don't use their brains
But let us always remember
Who put people in all of this rain

It wasn't a dog that peed on the floor
Or a cat that jumped on the table
It was people who turned their backs on me
That caused all of this trouble"

GOD MADE LOVE!

1976

The light from within
Dreamed upward shines
Into the night
Reflecting into the heart
And lighting the way
For a new day
To begin again

While the light from the stars
Opens the flower
Which is nourished
By a light toward a
More distant reality of love

God's Humble Servant

January 1, 2016

O God! Take pity on your humble servant
But let your will be done
Of your plan, help me to be observant
And do what is right by your Son

Walk with me in the dark forest
Ease my fear of death and destruction
May your angels sing their chorus
Please help me live by your instruction

May I drink wine that is your blood
And flee from all that is evil?
Awaken your flower from the bud
When it's lost, make my soul retrievable

May I hear your voice in your song?
Please help me live by your word
When I'm sick, make my spirit strong
And let your will be heard

God's Love is Vast
2010

I beseech you, O thou who
Are the Lord of all names
By your name through which
You have subdued all living things

Your servants and your loved ones fix
At all times upon your pleasure
For what you desire for humanity
Is God's greatest treasure

You are praiseworthy by humanity
Present, future and past
And are to be obeyed
For your love is vast

You look upon them who are dear
From your holy place
And send down for them alone
The profits of wisdom through your grace

GRASSY PLAINS
MAY 26, 2013

If the streets of heaven are not gold
I'll settle for the grassy plains
Somewhere I won't grow old
Anywhere in God's domain

Let me stay in his holy camp
I won't be in need of medicine
I'll make my way by Jesus' lamp
I won't need the light of Thomas Edison

I hope there is clean night air
Then I can sleep and I can dream
I'll dream I ride a white mare
I'll ride her 'round Saturn's rings

There is one thing I would pray for
That is above any other
I would head straight for her door
And have dinner with my mother

GREATEST JOY
2014

Jesus knew that he was soon to be betrayed
By a friend who cared no more for him than money to be made
But the tide soon turned leaving Judas' neck in a twist
And Iscariot's remembered for his part in all of this

Christ said, he without sin may cast the first stone
And try not to worry for the lilies don't
Forgive our trespasses as we forgive trespassers
And God is the power and glory forever

When the Savior was as dead as a fish in factory waste
His corpse was carried to its resting place
Mary Magdalene went to his tomb the Sunday after
Her greatest joy was the risen Master

Christ said, he without sin may cast the first stone
And try not to worry for the lilies don't
Forgive our tresspasses as we forgive trasspassers
And God is the power and glory forever

The Little Boy and the Big Fish
2005

Little Tommie Stout
Went down to the river
Soon he reeled a big fish out
To eat for his dinner

The fish begged him to refrain
He said he tasted bad
And it would be inhumane
And disturbing to the lad

It was a moving speech
A speech to leave one crying
So Tommie tossed the fish in the...
Grease
And left him frying

THE HOWL
FEBRUARY 25, 2014

In the distance, I heard a howl
Calling me to join their pack
It was followed by a growl
Just before I was attacked

On the mores of Britain
In the full moon light
Take care you are not bitten
Or there you'll stalk the night

Body parts found on the trails
What fiend could have done this?
Carry loved ones home in pales
Strange things are seen in the mist
A silver bullet through the heart
Will kill the beast for sure
But it's hard to tell that organ apart
Beneath all of that fur

I caught one and gave it a name
And trained it not to pee inside
But it ripped out the priest's jugular vein
Now the villagers have arrived

THE ROBE THAT WILL NOT WEAR OUT
JUNE 18, 2004

God said:

"I've placed in you the essence of my light
I've created you with my fingers of strength
What fear have you of perishing?
Why do you fear you'll become extinct?

You are of God's dominion and my dominion partner
Wherefore comes the fear you should perish?
You're a light that reflected from my soul to yours
A light I shall forever cherish

You are my glory, my glory fades not
You wear my robe, the robe of the devout
Abide by the Master
And you'll wear the robe that never wears out

Tell the children in the holy city
That paradise is within their grasp
Call on all immortal dwellers
Strive to unravel mysteries of the past

Eat wisdom from eternal fruit
And learn the secrets of the divine
Solaced are the eyes therein
As every soul is intertwined"

Wilted Flower

2013-12-26

I'm a mortal, born of woman
Full of doubt and full of trouble
I came up like a flower, now I'm wilted
With a gray beard of stubble

There is hope for a tree
Cut it down, it will sprout again
But when mortals die
What happens to us then?

Will the heavens open wide?
Will the dead rise again
And walk in a paradise
Unknown to living women and men?

When we die, will our minds
Turn completely into sand?
Are we good for nothing more
Than to fertilize the land?

Over time the mountain falls
The rain washes it away
But for now I'm a wilted flower
With a beard of gray

THE SONG CAPTAIN MIRACLE SANG TO HIS HORSE
1975

What is more reason?
Someone asked us to say so untrue
Are all secret wishes misdirected to you?
And where does it say we were all saved in time
To be ahead of our fate and succeed with this crime?

Its so called ambition has been lost now for years
So what is your life like as you break down in tears?
Does it grow you up tighter, does it make you a mess
If your friends misdirect you and see up your dress?

And what is so called
After whom and like what?
Am I certain I'm guessing
If I am, am I not?

These questions are many
Like few that I've seen
They make you grow senile
Instead of obscene

So with lack of a shirt
In my pocket I write
I laugh like a jackal
I hope I'm alright

May we return tomorrow and be mixed up again?
So see you are slowly, is it something I've been?
I then stared into my eyesight
It always sees me through

My days are feeling back again
And sometimes so do you

Then I heard my dreary drips
Calling me away
They said they were uncertain
So I carried them away
That is, until we're back!

OUR SON OF MAN
2014

Dwell not on hate and seek no revenge
Try to be brave and make foes our friends
Almighty God passes to Christ his sword
To conquer death and provide our reward

The Lord's word is light and easily understood
Do what is right and our fruits will be good
He tames the storm with his command
The Son of God and our Son of Man

We can't follow him and worship cash
Spiritual love is the kind that lasts
All worlds are his; seas and desert sand
The Son of God and our Son of Man

NEPTUNE'S SERENADE

AUGUST 10, 2012

Our love is never-ending
Not by days and nights we remember
But by ups and downs always bending
It lives by words soft and tender

Starfish falling in the sea
The moon is in our favorite phase
Mermaids sing in harmony
They sing for Neptune's serenade

I like to ride the waves
On my seahorse, Dapple Blue
I often save the day
I have little else to do

There is gold in treasure chests
They are found in sunken ships
And if you don't mind getting wet
We may get very rich

So much to see in every ocean
Myth and monsters yet discovered
Multicolored fish in motion
Baby whales being mothered

WATERED GARDEN
2012-11-01

for Lori

May your life become a watered garden
May you sing and dance in the heights
And like a firefly
Be radiant in the night

May you never want for kindness
Or for grain, wine or oil
May you always find happiness
In all you grow in the soil

Every time you reach out
May you lay your hand on true friends
May you never spend one moment
Among selfish women or men

May you be happy in your toil
May you find help when you ask
May you find the limelight
In which I know you like to bask

May you own a field of land
And it be green with grass and trees
And a pond with lily pads
And frogs, ducks and geese

Printed in the United States
By Bookmasters